Robert Burton Rodney

Alboin and Rosamond

Robert Burton Rodney

Alboin and Rosamond

ISBN/EAN: 9783744685108

Printed in Europe, USA, Canada, Australia, Japan

Cover: Foto ©Thomas Meinert / pixelio.de

More available books at **www.hansebooks.com**

AND

LESSER POEMS.

BY

ROBERT BURTON RODNEY
U. S. N.

———

PHILADELPHIA:
1870.

Entered, according to Act of Congress, in the year 1870, by

ROBERT BURTON RODNEY,

In the Clerk's Office of the District Court of the United States for the Eastern District of Pennsylvania.

A Memorial

BY HIS REMOTE SON,

TO

WILLIAM RODNEY OF RODNEY-STOKE,

IN THE COUNTY OF SOMERSET, ENGLAND.

DIED JUNE 10, 1669, AND BURIED IN HUNTSPILL CHURCH—THAT SHIRE.

A POET;

HIS MOTHER COUSIN-GERMAN TO EDWARD VI;

HIS FAMILY ANCIENT AND MANORIAL: ITS NORMAN

NAME,

SPOKEN WITH PRAISE AND TRUST BY KINGS AND PRESIDENTS;

AND IDENTIFIED WITH

ENGLISH GLORY AND AMERICAN LIBERTY.

From out a vault a flowering vine
    Escaled the minster buttress old:
Its crest was where the noonbeams shine;
    Its roots within the buried mould;
And from the hand-like sprays were thrown
Its blossoms on the tablet stone.

So, cherished sire, whose name I write,
    Thy humble muse revives in me:
'Tis nurtured in another light
    Of letters, grace and liberty;
But flowers which thy spirit gave,
Shall strew thy unforgotten grave!

CONTENTS.

	PAGE
Alboin and Rosamond	11
Rural Leisure	48
Odes. (Nos. 1 to 11)	61
The Blockade-Runner	77
A Seaside Dream	81
The Iceberg	92

NOTE.

THE story of Alboin and Rosamond is tersely narrated by Edward Gibbon, in that Twenty Years Task so worthy of his infinite learning and Corinthian majesty of mind.

The Poem at times traces the text, as a railroad the windings of river. Comparison will show where the writer strikes off into borders of incident, description, philosophy and morality: designing that these many stanzas, like the successive arches of a Campania aqueduct, bring the waters of truth from the far mountains of history.

R.

ALBOIN AND ROSAMOND.

WALKING Ravenna's streets one day,
    A quaint cathedral, old and dim;
With open doors beside the way,
    Allured me with its vesper hymn.

Few lingered in the nave; and I
    Knew not the language of the rite;
So crossing to a legend nigh,
    I read it by the failing light:—

A brazen-lettered slab of lead
    Did some red cardinal inhume;
A marble angel's wings outspread
    Deepened the shadow on the tomb:

While shrines ranged bright and tablets cold
    Within the aisles' columnar march;
And victory-gilded banners old
    Drooped from the frescoed transept arch.

But humbler grave I now espied:—
   A sunken sepulchre beyond,
Which bore upon its mouldering side
   The simple carving "Rosamond."

Soon the grey verger drawing near,
   With all dismissed, observed me then;
And while we twain sat lonely here,
   He told the history I pen.

ALBOIN the Lombard's prince and heir,
   The Gepidæ's in battle slew:
Loud to his sire men declare
   The Feast of Victory his due.

The monarch spake—"Our law must stand:
   No prince sits at his father's board,
Till he from foreign, royal hand,
   Receives his armor, spear and sword!"

Alboin in reverence bowed: he chose
   Forty companions; and his way
Took to the stronghold of his foes—
   The palace of the Gepidæ.

Their king with hospitable rite,
   Met the destroyer of his son,
Who at the banquet chanced that night
   To sit where sat the fallen one.

In Turisund sad longing wakes;
   That hoary host can but repine—
" How dear that seat the stranger takes;
   How hateful is this guest of mine!"

Flushed Cunimund, his living heir,
   With filial and fraternal fire :—
Fierce his quick sarcasm scorched the air,
   Fiercer a Lombard was replier:

All thundered up from o'erthrown seats,
   With raging crests and weapons' blaze;
But lo! what voice their names repeats,—
   What spell the dreadful typhoon stays?

"Observe the truce—let honor reign
   Although our hearts with torture bleed :
Bring me the armor of my slain;
   Give it the stranger—'twas his meed!"

Invested as he had aspired,
   Alboin was told to part in peace;

While aged Turisund retired,
   To wait in death his grief's surcease.

Thou wert Barbarian, history saith;
   But O with virtue, scorn of crimes,
With lowlier meekness, loftier faith,—
   To shame the thrones of polished times!

Now the departing guest to view,
   Looked Rosamond from out her bower:
The child of Cunimund he knew;
   And earth had cause to wail the hour.

His straggling spears toward home advance;
   But Alboin execrates his lot:
Lovelorn at one unhappy glance,
   Lo, all his honors are forgot;

And with them, his affianced bride
   Then waiting in St. Denis' nave:
Thus quickly he that troth denied,
   The House of Clovis slowly gave.

He nears his town on mountain shelf:
   How swift his drama's changes wing!—

His father's dead; and he himself
   Exalted on a shield, a king.

The Franks and Visigoths attend,
   Italia gratulation lifts,
Byzantines hides and jewels send;—
   Disguising tribute under gifts:

But slave of impulse—passion-mad,
   He loathes, he tramples on his good;
All sleepless till at last he had
   The royal maid by missive wooed.

On silk, with purple ink and lac,
   A captive Greek prepares the strain;
A noble bears it—brings it back—
   'Tis spit upon, 'tis wrenched in twain!

Stung with contempt, his wrath aglow,
   He leads and hurls his gathered hordes:
The Gepidæ repulse their foe,
   By succor from the Grecian swords.

O'erwhelmed with failure, war's fatigues,
   Bleeding with loss, his kingdom torn;—

Across a hundred ravaged leagues,
  He hears her silvery laugh of scorn.

———

REVENGE! thou whirlwind of the soul;
  Was thy arouser e'er devised,
Of steadier fervor, less control,
  Intenser force, than love despised?

Scorn of one's talents, conduct, lot,
  Or birth, may fortitude o'ercome;
But separate proffered self!—the shot,
  Through tenfold meekness, pierces home.

He only can withstand the smart,
  Who unto God refers his lot:
Divine decrees control the heart,
  And make it either love or not.

The man of prayer's complaint upwells
  Beneath that stroke, of strokes the worst;
"Turn my lost battle, Lord, or else
  Give me the peace I had at first!"

And even here it shall be proved—
  The sanctified, afflictive hour,

Was better boon than she beloved,
  With all the graces for her dower.

The spikenard vase, when broken, spread
  A heavenly fragrance all around;
But noxious things, when crushed, will shed
  Their secret poison on the ground:

So the proud hearts disdain to yield,
  Recoil on God who smote them low,
Brave the thick bosses of His shield;
  Fail or succeed—to greater woe.

With brain in baleful scheming deft,
  Alboin each last resource debates;
He looks around: allies are left;
  And the Avars he supplicates.

In haughty apathy they heard:—
  " Why should thy quarrel ours be made?"
Till by his abjectness bestirred,
  They name the recompense of aid:

"Tithe us thy nation's cattle now;
  And, be the Gepidæ subdued,
Then all their lands to us allow,
  With half the spoils and multitude!"

Again the ecstasy of wrath
  Comes on; and prompts compliance meek:—
"All that the Chagan names, he hath;
  And all thy avarice can seek!"

His eyes, far set on vengeance, spurn
  The care war's overture demands;
As fowler aiming at the erne,
  Heeds not the pitfalls where he stands.

Avars from pasture, hut and hunt,
  The whipcrack their war-signal own;
The thunderous horde, with fraying front,
  Invades the Gepidæ alone:

While Alboin his career deflects,
  And elsewhere enters with his few;
Whom reigning Cunimund selects
  The first in detail to pursue.

The Cæsar, angered at a slight,
  Sends no more succors from the East:
Vain Gepidæ no aid invite;
  And that of puerile Greeks the least.

Shall we trust Fortune?—death or bars
  O'erwhelm the confident and strong:

The sword trust?—it in duels, wars,
   Absolves and legalizes wrong:

Whom shall we trust?—whate'er our force,
   Whate'er our weakness, Prayer maintain:
Alas! 'tis empty woe's resource—
   Fullness neglects that potent strain.

Stanch Cunimund and host are lost;
   And chaliced, for two centuries gaze,
His skull aflame with golden cost,
   Grims wassail nights and festal days.

The bold and bad succeed; and why?—
   Faith is so precious in God's view,
Their recklessness He shames us by;
   Rewards their counterfeit as true.

Why wail, O heart, those freaks of Fate
   So many maxims have defined;
New coynesses of Chance relate,
   Call man uncertain, Fortune blind?

'Tis God elects our flush to mar,
   Or to despair joy's sequel bring;—

That He may teach us what we are,
   And prove Himself the only King!

To Rosamond went the conqueror;
   But not in pride, nor armor-clad:—
His step was lowlier than before,
   His garment mean, his aspect sad.

He pleaded war the sole device
   Of rulers then;—'twas equal chanced—
Her father might have triumphed twice,
   Her nation and not his advanced:

What oped the rivalry of blood—
   Was it not love? and if despair
Changed it to rage, he flung the good
   All at her feet—himself was there!

The royal orphan helpless stood—
   Her thoughts, anxieties she kept;
Yielded the hand her master sued;
   But with averted gesture wept:

And while the grass of peace resmoothed
   The hillocks of the fatal field

Her captive countrymen she soothed,
  Their needs abated, wounding healed.

Oft forests heard her hymn, her sob,—
  Alone there save her grandsire's shade:
It calmed resentment's burning throb.
  It made a chancel of the glade:

Yet in her form of radiant dust,
  A will awaited time's employ,—
Like sulphur 'neath the planet's crust,
  Reserved to shatter and destroy.

The Chagan gained his bloody due;
  For Transylvania his became,—
Moldavia and Wallachia too,
  And eastern Hungary; but the fame—

Fell to Alboin: him minstrels chose;
  His valor, largess, skill recall:—
In many tongues his songs arose,
  Till Charlemagne sought and re-wrote all.

Embossed around the ancient vase,
  Are scenes and heroes of its day:

When wrought, in quivering fire's enchase,
  They flecked the incandescent clay.

Soon cold and garlanded it lured
  Amid a villa's marble bloom;
And then two thousand years endured
  The breathless darkness of a tomb.

Moderns its tracery behold;
  But present cares diverting call;
And lone and sombre, gathering mould,
  It decks a transatlantic hall:

Till pensive child strays idly past:—
  Its marvels strike, its histories chain;
To him, as when in furnace cast,
  Those scenes and heroes glow again.

A virtue quits that object dumb;
  He feels its emulative thrill;—
That earth a power has become,
  Though to another earthy still.

So stands the Story of the Cross:—
  To worldly eye unmeaning, cold;
But in the child its truths engross,
  Inspires the saving faith of old.

Its simplest deed of love's more fair
   Than glory spread by minstrel bribed;
And the Redeemer's household Prayer,
   Than all the songs that kings transcribed.

Sunlight contains all colors: so
   With Faith,—all graces mingle here:—
Sorrow alone their hues can show—
   The only prism her crystal tear.

A BROKEN fount is mundane joy;
   And whoso drinks shall thirst again:
Soon, soon the zests of triumph cloy;
   And appetite revives its pain:

The heart inquires if all be got
   Of its imagined merit's due;
While each enhancement of the lot,
   Enhances that vain merit too.

But real cares made Alboin brood:—
   Profusion lasts and treasures fail:
Of Southern wealth and lassitude,
   He hears with eagerness the tale.

In the still depth the dolphin floats,
   Distending soft each gilded fin;
Nor the o'erbalanced sailor notes—
   Poising the deathful javelin:

So fair Italia in her plain,
   Thought not the restless Lombard's quest;
Till kneeling on her Alpine chain,
   He drove the arrow to her breast.

As lion from the rustling nook
   Steps out; and silent pausing stands;
The browsing flocks a moment look—
   Then fly the devastated lands;

So from the vineyards empty fled
   Esquire and gentle, tamed by ease;
While some unto the islets sped,
   And built the City of the Seas.

Throw wide the terraced pomp, where fruit
   And lilies mock the sick one's eye;
Parks where, while noble archers shoot,
   The needy can but look and die!

The smoke shall roll a denser black,
   From paintings rich with rainbows' spoil;

And paneled ceilings crisper crack,
With chiseled wreaths and glazing oil.

Unlock, unlock each haughty door;
And pride's adorned arcanums show!
They never opened to the poor;
And God shall ope them to the foe.

High at your feasts His sad ones put,
Nor deem the stranger to intrude;
For penury has a hallowing foot—
Exclude it and you Christ exclude.

The Voice that moved the prophet's pen,
Still speaks to luxury and sin :
Show mercy now, O happy men,
Before your mourning shall begin!

Ah those benignant hearts are each,
Forever rare, forever new;
Like amber on the pebbled beach;
And as the tears of rapture few.

Alboin that kingdom's map unrolled—
Effaced all titles, wrote again;
And LOMBARDY is still enscrolled,
Through every century, conquest, reign.

When the advanced and newly-crowned
   Survey their suitors, false and true;
Satan surpasses all around
   In skill to flatter, lead and sue.

With humble men his bands abate:
   He can endure the loss of those;
But with the great he rises great,
   And all his massing cohorts throws.

From weak ones, some deputed elf
   May the nefarious purpose gain;
But to the strong he goes himself—
   And few have heard his voice in vain:

"Devote to me your splendid trust—
   Your beauty, titles, wealth, applause;
Or if believe the Lord you must,
   At least be idle in His cause!"

"Go serve Him!" wily Pharaoh cries—
   "But leave your cattle—journeying far!"
Nor thinks the dupe, as he complies,
   The heart is where the treasures are.

He feels the mastering power of sin;
   And often strives to break the spell;

And then as oft falls back within
   The magnet gravity of hell :

Till in his mind, the Evil wraith
   Shuts off each light still holy there ;
Withers the listless hand of faith—
   Perpetual seals the lips of prayer.

O ye, with starry talents dight,
   Whose passions rage in generous war ;
Harness those mettled steeds of might,
   And bind them to Religion's car :

Serve God with all you are and own—
   Happy to pledge such chances vast ;
Before the rainbow-circled Throne,
   Rejoice that you have crowns to cast !

Hail heaven-devoted spirit !—would
   That we had more, our world to bless ;
To force the pathway, high and good,
   Through whole defeat and half success :

Let lower minds exult, despond,
   Or bide content with present deeds ;—
That clearer vision, set beyond,
   Alone to full achievement leads.

Relieved on classic marble wide,
   Legions parade the trophied ore,
Centurions look from side to side;
   But laureled Cæsar straight before.

A MANY-HOURED Autumn chase
   Had swept through rustling vineyards home;
For gaily dead to zeal and grace,
   The king his sportive miles must roam.

He drew his foamy bit to note
   The quarry, boar and wildfowl spoil;
And flung aside his leathern coat,
   With many a forest struggle's soil.

The grateful bath and linened ewer
   Prepared for evening feast and ease;
And moated lines entrenched secure
   That villa of a Veronese:

While the far owner mayhap gives
   Less thought to exile, want and pain,—
When hearing that a monarch lives
   Where she can never walk again.

So children of a noble stem
  View with odd principle of pride,
E'en a disease, if proving them
  To be by common blood allied.

Then larder, river, vault and vat
  Sent to the banquet all they may:
Along the oak the huntsmen sat;
  Their chief's eburnean chair midway.

Medals with emperors' brows embossed,
  Lay round his neck in golden rest;
A glittering sash of garnets crossed
  The tufted ermine of his breast:

To clothe his massive head aloft,
  Two foxes gave their pricking scalps;
And on the floor his shoon were soft
  In wolf skins of the higher Alps.

From his blue eye an instant sailed,
  As 'twere a squadron armed for fight;
And then, as pensive thought prevailed,
  It mellowed to poetic light.

No branching sconces darted fire
  Along the walls, with wearying glare;

Nor central candelabra's pyre
   Swung flashing in the withered air:

But from the ceiling to his chin,
   Cherubs let down a lamplet's chain—
Twelve burners lapped the oil within
   Twelve shells of bright, translucent stain.

So sweetly darkened is the hall,
   Its baffled splendors fitful glim,
Like bandits' sparry cave, when all
   Save each surrounding face is dim.

With rising riot, a fiend steeped
   Dormant in wine a century tunned;
To Alboin's mouth, from prison leaped,
   And cried "The skull of Cunimund!"

They brought the trophy set in gold,—
   The gems seen far before it came;
And in its sutured channel rolled
   Nectars of strange, provincial name:

The conqueror poured with every brand;
   And passed the cup for each to sip;—
Each first quaff mounting in his hand,
   The last returning to his lip:

Till with the long excess aglow,
    He seized the bowl with altered voice—
"This to the queen, that I may know
    She with her sire and us rejoice!"

He filled it to the topmost line,
    While all sat round in full-eyed hush;
But hark! the gurgling of the wine
    Is like the life-blood's throttling gush;

And as he swung it to the groom,
    It spilt with many a plash and stain;
And a thin smoke arose, as from
    A mangled soldier instant slain.

The stripling trembles, as with lips
    In superstitious fright apart;
Away he bears it, as it drips,
    And hands the queen a broken heart:

For with a wail which faintings break,
    She sees the mournful token come;
And hears the message Alboin spake;
    And dips her lips with horror numb.

Submissive words go softly back
    With that dread chalice to the hall;

But now a storm is fringing black;
   And darker drops than tears must fall:

For she could many a wrong relate,
   Unexpiated by renown;
And sufferance brave had changed to hate—
   Unsoothed by a divided crown:

And this his closing stroke of shame!
   But soon along the terraced path,
Her favorite guard, Helmichis, came—
   Summoned to serve her fatal wrath.

The whispered crime wakes no alarms;
   No oath of reticence occurs;—
Held firmly by those matchless charms,
   His mind is the reflex of hers:

But the war king to meet alone!—
   It forces death-damp to the brow:
One only is his equal known,
   Whose aid they dare petition now:

So, through her minion sent to sue,
   She stalwart Peredéus tried;
But the camp's champion, grimly true,
   Her every plea and bribe denied.

A thought was left—amid her train
   Was one with him an amour led:
That night, a night of gloom and rain,
   She chose whose humbler place instead:

The guilty truth Helmichis made
   The warrior know, when noon was high:—
"Fulfill her mandate, or betrayed,
   At sunset thou art led to die!"

So, self-devoted, naught can shock—
   No sacrifice dismay her more:
As one would kneeling at the block,
   Strip the last priceless gem he wore.

The traitor guardsmen, at a wheel
   In secret by each other turned;
Whetted anew their heavy steel;
   And loitered till her plan they learned.

The eve was coming on; and glad
   Upon a tranquil couch to fall;
His brow with vanished transport sad,
   The husband sought her lonely hall.

She brushed his glossy, flaxen crown;
  Peered in his swimming eyes of blue;
Moistened his burning cheeks; and down
  His mane-like beard, her comb she drew:

And from her pearly fan evolved,
  The zephyrs waved his forehead's tress;
Her silk, imbued with flowers resolved,
  Shook fragrance round each fond caress.

The drowsy monarch thus ensnared,
  Forgot the fever of the day;
Forgot his orgied insult dared;
  And brokenly she heard him say—

"Beside the rugged life I led,
  How sweetly paid my toils have been:
How bright my captured cities spread,
  When I remember thee, O queen!

"I sometimes dread the chance of war
  Will reave me of these valleys green;
But I'll range wide to conquer more
  For thee, loved Rosamond, O queen!"

No more can this her bent restrain,
  Than iron, white with flames below;

Cooled by a passing gust of rain,
   Can fail resume its deathly glow.

Preparing for the fell assault,
   No sound, no sign, her presence gave :—
Like the miasma of a vault,
   She floated o'er the matted pave :

Till every artifice bethought,
   Defence, escape or aid to foil ;
The tall and splendid door she sought—
   Its golden hinges dripped with oil.

Shrunk half their size, her lurking imps
   Cross on furred feet the darkened scene ;
The mirrors catch their creeping glimpse ;
   They pass the purple couch's screen :

King, warrior, reveler—there he lay—
   Flung back like one in battle slain ;
And steeped in crimson light—a ray
   Bursting through shrouded oriel pane.

Thus far they moved ; but Helmichis
   Convulsive faltered, turned to speed :—
"Stay ! slay !" she gasped with cobra hiss—
   "Or I arouse him ; and ye bleed !"

They struck like madmen:—hand at hilt,
  He rose as one no terrors quell;—
His sword is fastened by her guilt;
  And struggling it to draw, he fell.

A consul's lofty altar-tomb
  Far in the park its sculptures hid;
And there in torchless dark they come—
  To lift and close the echoing lid:

Within, the red of crime prevailed;
  Without, the green of moss and fern;—
A soaring eagle, arrow-paled,
  Marbled forever on the urn.

NATIONS' affairs must yet proceed
  Be councils scattered, rulers slain;
The steeds of power resistless speed,
  Be hand or not upon their rein.

Majestic post—exalted trust!—
  To guide the coursers as they fly:
Surely the task well quitted must
  Gain brightest recompense on high.

O thoughtless is the choice they cast,
  Who crowd, uncalled, that sphere of care—
Seize without God those duties vast,
  His grace alone can teach them bear!

Twelve days held Rosamond the sway—
  Her throne upraised in tumult wild:
Around its base her Gepidæ;
  Upon its stair her princess-child.

Till closing in, like air so dense,
  Dispelled by bursting magazine;
The rallying chiefs the siege commence:—
  "Hurl from the barriers this queen!"

But now the happy Po so nigh,
  Looks o'er his margin tendering aid;
Holding to Rosamond, fain to fly,
  Barges for former princes made:

Then in the breezy gloom she sails,
  With coffered spoils and guardsmen tried;—
East till the second morn unveils
  The Adrian estuary wide.

The air grows strangely fresh, and lulls
  The throbbing nerves; the mirrors show

The offing of blue mist—the gulls
    Skimming across like shells of snow;

The headlands dim in distant parts,
    With here and there a sail to fleck;
The pilots, scattering with their charts,
    Bright instruments upon the deck.

Her own vexillum, furled before,
    Floats on the tall stem-planted spear;
And cheering crew, with mast and oar,
    Now southward for Ravenna steer:—

Stronghold of Greco-Roman hope,
    While Cimbrian hoofs swept far the lands;
And Tiber's bride was forced to ope
    Her forum to the spoiler's hands.

Behind its marshes, forts and sea,
    Young Honorius slept in down;
When chastely gentle, e'en as he,
    His brother wore the Eastern crown.

Here Stilicho his armor kept;
    Here Belisarius victor came;
And Narses from a harem stept,
    To change obscurity to fame.

Ravenna slowly glides to view
  Beyond its barring lines and mole:
The queen perplexed and fearful too,
  Scans from the prow her only goal:

Like bubble blown by Titan child,
  A soaring dome presides o'er all;—
The vapors of the gulf and wild,
  Condensing on its mighty ball:

And smaller, but of equal craft,
  Loom at its side a beauteous twain—
On many a white pilastered shaft,
  A golden angel at each vane.

From marts replete with myriad wares;
  Shipping and wheels and hammer-blows;
From baths and camps and endless squares;
  The city's sea-like murmur rose.

On the canal's defended quay,
  Her barges grate; the gates divide,
Ope up the long perspective way,
  With palaces on either side.

On a triumphal arch's crest,
  A warrior drove with whirlwind speed—

Six giant horses pranced abreast;—
    But struck in bronze was every steed.

Winged o'er a lofty pillar's frieze,
    A pausing god his footstep set;
And at the founts the sundown breeze
    Blew rainbow showers from every jet.

For new frivolity or home,
    Leaving ten thousand marble seats;
And streaming from the hippodrome,
    The gaudy peoples choked the streets:

Where Christians came from other climes,
    There to admire, lavish, dwell;
Where glory glossed the prince's crimes;
    And flowers hid the mouth of hell.

They sought the Baal of the world,
    Were zealous but for him alone:
Vainly was priestly incense curled—
    The prayer addressed, the organ blown:

With them a dead belief sufficed;
    They sighed not for the heavenly rest;
They dreaded the reproach of Christ—
    Nor watched His coming with the blest.

O patient God!—to sit controlled,
  While to rebellion mortal lends
Thy very gifts of skill and gold,
  Of health and leisure, youth and friends.

With brilliant dress what woes began—
  How is the scorpion, not the dove,
That beauty given to soften man ;
  And win his heart to faithful love !

His lustful eye God's wrath invites ;
  But say, shall she by whom he's thralled,
Whose needless elegance incites—
  O say, shall she be guiltless called ?

Then tremble vernant fair one, lest
  Your glance become a poisoned barb ;
And clothe a Savior-loving breast,
  In sober hues and simple garb :

For as the summer evening's gust
  Smites the vile fume of earth away ;
The lightnings of His vengeance just,
  Shall close the world's long, sultry day !

Now far along the thronging road,
    Her charioteers slacked down the strings
At Cæsar's gate; where then abode
    Longinus, exarch, peer of kings.

The wary ruler all had heard;
    And curious now to see his guest,
Impatiently that eve deferred;
    But 'twas his morning's first behest:

And soon the prayerless morning shone;
    The sparkling court drew out array,
The aureate halls were open thrown;
    And flowered crimson spread her way.

The outlines of that wondrous face
    Anew in guileless mould were cast:
Of her ill deeds as free from trace
    As ocean of the tempests past.

While she advanced through light and shade,
    Her eye of varying color seemed:
As grey, as sea blue, brown, it played;
    And then an agate hazel gleamed.

In white, with golden sash and hem,
    Her temples cool with forest flower;

A mazarine train—and over them
   The candid confidence of power.

"Hail famous queen! enjoy thou long,
   While nations war, Ravenna's peace—
Siege-proof and splendor-built; with triremes
     strong,
   And arms of Asia, Thrace and Greece!"

Then flashed her smile—the light that rays
   From whirling wheels of chariot cars:
Her blush the deepening hue that plays
   Athwart the twinkling disc of Mars:

And her weird eye, with lustre filled,
   O'er Longinus potential roved;
For ere he spake his blood was thrilled;
   And ere he ceased the exarch loved.

Soon from the palace depths her spell
   Upbreathes to sway the counciled throne;
Her features in new frescoes dwell,
   Are in remoulded bronzes shown.

An emperor made Ravenna grand;
   But were Honorius reigning then,
His passive soul had burst command;
   And he had loved like other men!

Death hovers always near to love;
   And every curse seeks ambush there:
As gaudiest Bengal arbors prove
   The fever's, cobra's, tiger's lair.

Let man deny himself; for our
   Exemplar self-denying came;
Nor, mad to gain lost Eden's bower,
   Rush on the angel's sword of flame.

While sensual Peredéus sips
   Each courtly joy with reckless zest;
Above a fountain's marble lips,
   Helmichis droops a scowling crest.

She marked his jealous wrath; forecast
   Peril from tool grown useless now;
Hindrance to hopes new opening vast,
   Like seas to the explorer's prow.

Oft brought she when from baths he stept,
   Urns of reviving nectar full;
And, fanned with smiles, suspicion slept,
   As one whom wings of vampyre lull.

So once when drinking gaily here,
   His ears in dreadful tocsin sang—

His breath closed short — the truth flashed
    clear—
Despair o'erruled his mortal pang:

Dying, he hurled her to the wall—
    He tore apart her tight-set teeth;
And down her gasping throat made all
    The chalice's remainder seethe:

Death swelled her veins; she sped her track
    Stifled with horrors of the tomb—
Her guilty brow with poison black,
    She reached the crowded presence-room.

The exarch started from his throne,
    Swept down the lictored steps of pride,
Dashed through the breathless hall alone;
    And in his frantic arms she died.

SHIPPED for Byzantium all her spoils,
    Her princess-child, her guards and he,
The Lombard victim of her toils;
    Sailed down the Adriatic sea.

Round Grecian capes their canvas swells;
    They thread Ægean isles and foam,
They pass the swarming Dardanelles;
    And kneel 'neath St. Sophia's dome.

The heiress-girl in convent died;
    And Peredéus, Samson-thewed,
With the arena's champions vied,
    Till prince and court with terror viewed.

They blinded him—lest hap perchance
    He'd rise and seize on power supreme;
And pricked by servile, Syrian lance,
    He dug the channel of a stream.

Cast out in age, with earning lyre,
    He sang to those of legends fond,
That tale of battle, love and ire—
    Of Alboin and of Rosamond.

The tale another's theme became—
    Once more by modest minstrel tried;
And still the hearers are the same,
    Though centuries and seas divide:—

The proud course on with careless brow ;
  And Christians, still, them homage give ;
Few, few the searching voice allow—
  " Is the world holier that I live?"

Some curse the rising sun ; and try
  To take the world to night agen ;
Or see with a complacent eye,
  The inequalities of men.

Haste on, O God, the great Release—
  Of all earth's hopes the only sure ;
For all its wars the only peace ;
  For all its woes the only cure :

Give saints the land whose light they court—
  Their perfect praise will sooner soar :
Cut the vain lives of bad men short—
  They'll have the less to answer for.

Haste on, O God, the great Redress—
  Let Satan in the pit be hurled ;
And cast into Thy streaming press,
  The mighty vintage of the world !

Finis

A. and R.

RURAL LEISURE.

A SYLVAN dame with face of tan,
Hails me, the travel-tarnished man;
    And I shall be her guest.
A larger log is on her fire;
And on the bed when I retire,
    Fresh linen from her chest.

Enlivening are her artless words;
Diversions all her place affords,
    She urges me receive:
The horse, the gun, the boat I choose:
These shall my holidays amuse—
    My morning, noon and eve.

Dear friend I'm thirsting—and you fill
From dairy can and orchard still,
    Your calices of wood:

RURAL LEISURE.

Dear friend I'm hungering—and you take
Your pantry's sauce, your barrel's cake,
    And finest of your brood.

But other fare I mean and need:
In dovecote homes what can exceed
    The joy of tranquil men?
Hope, wisdom, rest—my spirit teach
To look to God alone for each;
    And I grow cheerful then.

O with my Savior's love and thine,
Why should I for another's pine,
    In these unthankful bask?
Another's love I toil to gain;
But these come like the summer's rain—
    Acceptance only ask!

My sprightly bay, with zest and pride,
I daily haste to groom and ride:
Flushing with ardor from his grain,
He longs for sunshine, road and rein.
He's for my summer pastime lent;
And with my corn and blades content:

·Willing to traverse far for these,
And speed where'er I guide or please :—
The morning jaunt, the sportful chase,
Umbrageous lane or country race.

At daybreak on the road he serves,
In easy amble round its curves;
Meeting while yet the sky is dark,
The teamster with his load of bark
Or staves or wood—a compact heap
Brought far to be disposed of cheap.
The man (who walks) looks hard at me;
And would not know me could he see;
Yet still he eyes intently;—but
Down goes his wheel in sunken rut.

And now we have a scene of trouble :
The oxen strain with vigor double,
The single horse that heads the team,
Tugs and exerts till in a steam.
But no! the cumbrous burden bides;
And as to aggravate besides,
Come jug and dinner from the top,
Breaking and wasting as they drop:
He plies his shoulder, tears his clothes;
And falls back in a storm of oaths.

RURAL LEISURE.

At once I offer all I can—
My horse to pacify the man:
Spare collar, swingle-tree and chains,
He gratefully adjusts with pains;
Then pushes with his utmost strength,
While I dispense the lash's length:
The vexing forewheel now we start;
And with momentum we impart,
The hinder safely follows slow;
Then, freeing horse, I mount and go.

Meanwhile the objects of the land
Come into view on every hand;
Extinguished is the farmer's light
That made his window beacon night.
With sun-forerunning tints subdued,
The sky is silently imbued;
While tree and house and chimney trace
Their profiled outlines on its base;
And countless plants exhale anew
The subtle fragrancies of dew.

An osprey's nest for many a year,
Has been familiar landmark here;
Held high from scrutiny and harm
In an old poplar's withered arm.

The bird arouses while I gaze,
His wing in spiral flight essays;
Circling at lofty poise he floats,
And on the atlased township gloats;
Then plunges to his roofless house,
And nestles by his watching spouse.

The carpets of the household loom
Adorn the wayside tenant's room;
And through his doorway and his vine,
I see his furniture of pine;
His gun, with dingy tube and breech,
Swung up above his urchins' reach:
The mantel shelving trimly looks,
Laden with fan and clock and books;
While his poor wife rubs up with care,
The lately sullied breakfast ware.

And in the corner is the bed,
With laceless pillows at its head;
And gay with quilt composed perhaps
Of half an age's treasured scraps.
The trundle that on casters rolls,
Receives at night the little souls;
While overhead the rumbling feet
Betray the larger boys' retreat:

That narrow roof of lowly comb
Shields, after all, a cherished home.

Three wagons bring a picnic troop,
Each with its closely-seated group;
Going in all their country pomp,
To gather berries, climb and romp.
There glisten collar, coat and belt,
The ribboned hats of straw and felt,
The manto, parasol and hood,
White-napkined stores of dainty food;
And on before them jubilant,
The guiding negroes dance and chant.

Then by the neighboring coast again,
I mark the fishers draw their seine;
Drag up the shore the struggling mass,
And then the prizes sort and class:
At leisure view and value each,
Casting the tiny round the beach.
Poor innocents! they writhe and die—
Sand in the scale and in the eye;
While with their sullen oxen brown,
The vending carters seek the town.

When from the ships so long immuring,
  I flee and scent the forest dews;
Upon my arm my gun securing,
  I lonely saunter, idly muse.
I think again of fancies airy,
  Of states of life for which I've yearned;
While from my lips involuntary,
  Come the old woodland rhymes I've learned.

Here is a bridge whose warping sleepers
  The hasty chopper flung across;
And near it unsupported creepers
  Gushing their blossoms on the moss.
No more in reverie delaying,
  My falcon-hunting course I take;
And whistling back my dog from straying,
  Press on through undergrowth and brake.

  In the dank recess of the dell,
The centred rills their waters swell;
Then threading on through alder gate,
The basin daily renovate:
Their happy purling broke alone
By the crow's distant monotone.

Here crowd the shrubs of dampness fond,
And floating dock leaves pave the pond ;
The jay and redbird build the nest,
As sure no peril will molest ;
For quite too low for tearing squall,
Too dull to tempt the rustic's call,
Too hidden for migrating duck
His swarm to halt its herbs to pluck ;
This lakelet through the summers will
Abide unvisited and still.

But when the pirate falcon made
His haunt of this secluded glade,
Alarm the warbling tenants took,
And fled the devastated nook.
On an elm's shaggy bough halfway,
He wove his fagots, grass and clay :
His ambuscade the foliage wreath,
His castle-moat the pool beneath ;
While up the moisture-dripping stock,
Abattis vines their thorns enlock :
Secure the proud marauder seems,
And peals elate his taunting screams.

In truth he is a princely bird !
A nimbler wing was never stirred,

Acuter eye ne'er searched the plain,
Nor sharper talon pierced the brain:
With dark-blue plumage, speckled breast,
Long caudal quills and flattened crest,
A spur-won knight of bravest port,
At old king Eagle's forest court.
Not high gyrating ere he stoop,
He meditates the fatal swoop,
While his bale shadow 'gins to warn
And chicks fly under house or barn;
But skimming low he smites his food
From out some unsuspecting brood,
Ere lazy cock can sound alarm,
Or gunning boy prevent the harm.
The remnant scatter; and the bird
Feasts in the grass, unseen, unheard,
Till drips from off his rounded beak
The last blood-drop his rage can eke:
Then hieing to his guarded nest,
Enjoys the rapined meal digest;
And on the eggs all rough and blotch,
While speeds his mate, keeps warmth and
    watch.

    The months depart; and winter beats
Into the old abandoned seats:

The falcon-barons all have flown,
Chasing the flocks to milder zone.
They riot; and with heavy wing,
Their northern castles seek in spring.

My lanneret is bleeding now!
Shot down from off his lofty bough;
But ere he yields to pain and dies,
Throws wide his iris and defies.
Poor bird! we thy fell skill condemn;
But laud the same when seen in men:
The diadem by havoc won,
With glory cinctures sire and son.

For new pastime I'm ready:
　Let my yacht be the boon;
Have the gale mild and steady,
　And the time afternoon.
As glad as the springbok
　On his broad desert ground,
Casting off from the ringblock
　I course the blue sound.

As onward she verges
　　What harmony now!
For the music of surges
　　Is under the prow:
And buoyant, delicious,
　　The snowy clouds are;
And the storm unpropitious
　　Is absent and far.

The food-seeking plover
　　Darts by as I go;
The ospray pair hover,
　　The trout frisks below;
The headlands sand-bleaching,
　　Recede on the lee;
For swiftly I'm reaching
　　The inlet and sea.

We come on like the arrow!
　　I dextrously steer:
Here 'tis shallow, there narrow—
　　Hurrah!—and we're clear.
Now the sea wind romantic
　　Strains tenser my sail;
And laves the Atlantic
　　My dipping gunwale.

Behind me paraded
  The corn-harvests stand;
And bosky and faded
  The marshes expand;
While the cape's yellow margin
  Is seen o'er the spume;
And before me enlarging,
  The merchantmen loom.

Some outwardly bearing,
  Taut, tidy and strong;
Some scathed with the wearing
  Of voyages long;
And o'er the way watered,
  The figureheads weep,
For the drowned and the slaughtered,
  With the spray of the deep.

The eye of Henlopen
  Two leagues to the north,
Day-closed, now is open,
  And radiates forth:
Sad shades gain existence
  The ocean to rim;
And the ships of the distance
  In vapor are dim.

But still in sport venial
  My flight I maintain:
The eve is so genial,
  And morrows bring rain.
As the amateur skater
  Will gambol on steel,
The young navigator
  Delights on his keel.

Now out peeps the starlet,
  The crescent half shines,
The sunset's last scarlet
  Is streaking the pines.
Wearing round and retracing,
  I the miles slower run;
For the gale fresh and bracing,
  Has gone down with the sun.

And when the sail slacking,
  Is furléd and· fast;
Performed all its tacking,
  And home is at last;—
Then for banquet and slipper,
  For hearth and for glee;
And dreams of my clipper,
  The sound and the sea!

ODES.

ODE 1.

Could I a noble epic pen,
  Well fit to win the world's applause,
To you I would submit it,—then
  If need be, to the furnace jaws.

I would not mourn my fruitless pains,
  If only you had read each word;
Nor deem composed for naught the strains,
  If only you approving heard!

ODE 2.

Fair songstress! soon you will have read
  A stranger's lines; who sought this scene
Upon a conquering army's tread:
  Of lowly rank and homely mien.

He joys in psalmody of old,
  Admires its dulcet rendering;

And to the capable is bold,
  As now, in homage tendering.

Your home and virtues, race and lot,
  Are all unknown—your very name:
With him, howe'er, it matters not—
  You have his love and prayers the same.

No hope is his to enter free
  Your presence bland, and call you friend:
So undesirable is he,—
  Know him, your interest will end.

But this he trusts—your choral arts
  From holy motives all proceed;
The chants you warble be your heart's,
  And that you sing God's praise indeed.

Your face, your grace, your voice, are dower
  Well worthy gratitude: O then
Adore that God who gave you power
  To charm with these the souls of men!

ODE 3.

Strolling I noticed an abandoned gun,
Its breech and trunnions bedded in the loam:
The sod was sprouting o'er that grisly ton
Corroding in the elements; its chamber erst
Death harbored in, and whence he burst,
Like Coliséum lion, now the insect's home:
The sparrow sought a building-site to win;
And, chirping round the muzzle, peeped within.

I had indifferent passed the object by—
But in the circle of its silent mouth,
A flower fastened my discursive eye!
Pleasing it was; and all the more so there,
Without the rivalry of a parterre:
No gardener's sprinkle cherished it from drouth;
It drew its blue from mould and moisture scant;
For God will nurse and keep as well as plant.

It seemed, I thought, a shadowy type of her
Who is to me this castle's only lure:
In calm seclusion blooming, as it were,
Within the jaws of war; her gentle grace

The more observable in such a place:
But peace assures:—at its afflatus pure
A thousand reconciled extremes abound;
And the lambs frisk upon the battery's mound.

Yet, as the flower I could not pluck, nor long
Delay to contemplate,—so 'tis with thee!
My interest is passive, howe'er strong:
For I've renounced society's delights;
But thee to me a heavenly tie unites,
More durable than earth's affinity:—
My twin believer!—Christ by both adored—
Co-heir of hope—my sister in the Lord!

- ODE 4.

Dare custom primly bar,
Because a wife you are,
My eulogy?—at censorship I smile:
Lady! I'm ravished quite;
But mine's a guileless sight,
In roaming round this harmful world the while.

As ranged o'er valley great
With many a hedged estate,
The pilgrim's orb claims each, the nonce, its own;
Æsthetic none the less
Than if I did possess,
I prize all excellencies seen or known.

For human beauty true,
And nature's splendors too,
Are adumbrations of my God above;—
His witnessings, though dim,
That glory may to Him
Ascend from those who e'er admire or love.

Men might not sink so low,
Did woman alway show
That folly her incensement would ensure;
Nor license so entice,
Were the penalty of vice
Exclusion from the beauteous and the pure.

I know naught of your past,
Save that you must have cast
A radiance sweeter still—could such one see;
And soon I leave this spot,
To mark your future not;—
The present picture shall my memory's be.

But, lady, I'll allow
One cause I laud you, now:—
You image her whose hand I long to sue!
Unnumbered leagues away—
She is with me on the day
When I my courted vision have of you!

ODE 5.

As long as earth supplies her ores,
    Cast them, O artisan, in bells!
And, mason, while the rock is yours,
    Erect the tower where rapture dwells;
And through its mullioned windows pours
    Far floating peals and chants and knells!

It was an abbey's chimes so deep,
    Rolling on Neustria's blast;
That broke her conquering William's sleep,
    His dying and his last;
And 'mid their wild melodious sweep,
    His warlike spirit passed.

On what events before and since,
    In various lands the bell has rung!

And there have been the great—the prince,
　Remembered but through bells they hung:
A Schiller, as memoirs evince,
　Remembered by The Bell he sung.

But precious were those tones to me
　Which drew you from your father's hall:
My weekly glimpse of you, fair E——,
　Depended on their Sabbath call;
As sad I hovered—you to see—
　Along the church's ivied wall!

ODE 6.

From social conversation flown
To nurse a morbid grief alone,
I thought, from love and hope exempt,
Nothing remained return to tempt;
But some whom I at times have met,
Make me reflect if not regret;
Cause me to think my course is not
(As deemed) a God-appointed lot;—
And 'neath the moving glance of those,
Question the banishment I chose.

And you are one!—but how or why?
Perhaps concernment in your eye
I read; or felt myself and mood
By intuition understood;
And grateful for such kindness shown,
The freer did your merit own;—
Or by some sympathy divined
The touch of a superior mind:
Howe'er it be, the tale no less
Of admiration I confess.

Your classic face is cherished now,—
Revered—as is a royal brow:—
A mould too noble, unknown maid,
From my delighted mind to fade;
A cast unmarred by passion rash,
Frivolity's debasing flash,
Deception's artifice;—for truth
Seems to enhance your brilliant youth:
Your countenance my criterion stays,
By which all others to condemn or praise.

But why should I your presence dare,
For transitory rapture there?
Soon you depart—and I am more
Unblest, unhappy than before.

Parting my patience so transcends,
I have to shun the joys it ends;
And tread my sombre path of loss,
Accepting exile as my cross.
Some brighter destiny is thine:
Then follow it—I follow mine!

ODE 7.

A BEAUTY on a frosty morn
  Strolled outward for a walk;
Met a poor, shivering lad forlorn;
  And deigned with him to talk.

The boy looked up—her sympathy
  Had all his pain beguiled:
"Am I not cold? you ask"—said he—
  "I was, until you smiled!"

ODE 8.

Upon the ocean I would live and die;
  I would not part with it for beauty's hand:
There freedom rides health-teeming gales; and I
  Leave gloom and idleness upon the land.
The vastness satisfies my restless soul;
  With many scenes my heart and thoughts
    expand;
With God so near no creature need condole;
And human idols cease their fell control.

Soon I'm to hide behind its mist and mile;
  In the manned cutter off again to shove:
Adventure in some foreign realm or isle,
  May dim to soberness the tints of love.
But as the mighty plays of time unfold;
  And death and change and angels, good and
    vile,
Fight o'er the world,—I yearn still to behold
Joy's chaplet lustrous round your tress of gold.

Affecting presence!—that of naiad, elf,
   Or king, I fancy aweless;—this almost divine;
For having no infirmities yourself,
   How can you feel a charity for mine?
I've met unflinchingly death's chilly stare;
   But falter under yours without design:
Distrust of what my destiny may bear,
Comes on to prompt my proneness to despair.

Indifference the wily suitor feigns;
   At ease he sets your apprehensive eye;
He shows—whate'er the flame his breast contains—
   Only as much as he can profit by.
Spite woman's vaunted shrewdness and what not,
   She rarely foils the worldly courtier's pains.
I know all this; but who slacks to a trot
His rein, when folly's steeple-chase is hot?

It may not pleasure you or yours to make
   Disclosure thus, and choose so warm a tone;
But for relief I must my offering take,
   And lay it down at your ideal throne.
Proud girl! you shall know all, for candor's sake:
   I cannot be at peace my worship still unknown:

At every hazard, every risk, I'll prate;
And dare all odds for loveliness so great.

At various place the comely and refined
    Gave me their welcome; but my heart as now
Owned you its primal impulse—your high mind,
    Your peerless form and etiolated brow.
Think me not recreant, inconstant too,
    Accepting solace absence would allow;
That chancing your faint semblances to view,
I caught at them as imagery of you.

In sighs upon the faded little day
    In which 'twas mine to know you, ends my ode;
But that shall be to me when far away,
    Of all my memories dearest episode:
Your picture in my mind the treasured one,
    With that grand hill befitting your abode;
And its flecked valley spread in cloudless sun,—
Meet scene for eyes like yours to rest upon!

ODE 9.

When passing near an ancient tree,
    I sometimes quit the way,
To claim what blessing there may be
    Thereon my hand to lay.

And when the shoremen draw the net,
    And ply the string and knife;
I love to buy some struggling pet,
    And fling it back to life.

I love to stroke the roadside beast,
    Whose orbs inquire why:
Would that he were from toil released;
    Would that he were as I.

O would that all despised, oppressed,
    All ignorant and poor,
Become the equals of the best;
    And enter heaven's door:

Equals in lore and virtue—meet
    To walk with the refined;
Equals, not in their own conceit,
    But gesture, heart and mind.

In this lost world of ours, then,
    Let each that good devise:
The lover of his fellow-men
    Delights to help them rise.

He sullen caste must needful call;
    But needful evil 'tis:
He would not to vile levels fall;
    But lift them thence to his.

O Freedom! in thy zenith beam
    My soul forever feasts;
And musing on thy higher theme
    I've left the trees and beasts.

The beauty of the Godhead lurks
    In these, however dim;
And pleasure in His humbler works,
    Is pleasure found in Him.

ODE 10.

You smile on me!—perhaps if I should ask
To be made known to you, decorum's doors would
    ope ;
And at your side I'd be the chatting friend :—
Looking aloof with a complacent pity,
At those with lots or intellects so mean and low
And so debased, they be perforce denied
Your blest society for aye. Then were I struck
With want or woe or death, I'd have a claim
Upon your thoughts and sympathy ; and 'mid your
    pleasures,
The heart and time might come to speak of me.
But I'll forego all this—surrender all—
For the delicious dream of thinking you immortal !
Still let your hazel eye, replete with mysteries,
Shoot its far glance at mine ; your o'erheard voice
Move me as would a monarch's ; and the walks,
Where you have been in flower-encircled hat
And garb of white with sea-blue hem, be, by
Your loitering there, forever hallowed ; and your
    presence
To me as awful as a lonely forest nook
Illumined by the summer moon at midnight !

ODE 11.

THERE is a gallery of portraits rare
Within my memory, to which I oft repair
    In lone reflection.

These are the etchings of the perfect few
Whom I have met; who from my spirit drew
    Praise or affection.

Within that gallery there is a niche,
Which tracery of you shall soon enrich;—
    Sweet, latest Recollection!

THE BLOCKADE-RUNNER.

The morning fog is clearing now:—
"A sail upon the starboard bow!"
The eagled youths who idling pass,
Consult the quartermaster's glass;
Up springs the officer-of-the-deck;
The message boy speeds at his beck,
To where the Captain in the stern
Awaits such merry news to learn.
The gunboat to the point is brought,
The aiding sails are sheeted taut,
The red-mouthed funnels windward set,
The firemen at the furnace sweat;
Roundly the quickened paddle spins;
And with a cheer the chase begins.

The stranger marks afar the scheme;
And likewise crowds his sail and steam:
The breeze is faint; but canvas spread
May drive the ship a knot ahead.

The double stacks begrime and choke;
Disgorging streams of gloomy smoke,
Which rising in the sultry air,
Form ebon clouds that dally there:
And plainly to the most unskilled
Appears the vessel's British build:—
Long, low and narrow, wheels aside,
Brig-rigged, and made upon the Clyde;
The fore-peak housed, a taffrail staff
For flags which elsewhere climb the gaff;
The masts and chimneys raking back;
The hull daubed grey instead of black:—
To run unseen at dawn and eve,
Or by that Federal hue deceive.

And gradual as the noontide wanes,
The active cruiser toils and gains;
For hours along the sunny deeps
She quivers on with willing leaps;
While o'er the stubborn shafts supreme,
Dances the glittering walking-beam;
As tossing high its burnished cups,
From which each joint its oiling sups;
And faithful plying, void of noise,
It oscillates on graceful poise.
The sails they wet, the ballast shift,
To trim for steady flight more swift;

And hoisted from the lower hold,
Tierces of pork are nimbly rolled,—
Torn from its crashing staves and tires,
Hurled sputtering in the furnace fires.
Man after man no longer copes
With that fierce heat,—drawn up by ropes,
And stretched on deck but half alive,
Water is dashed, them to revive:
All are exhausted by the blaze:—
Seamen must come and work relays.

"Stand by your forward rifled gun—
Blank cartridge first, but only one!"
With puff and flame the roar rings out,
Nor puts the fugitive about:
Then earnest fire—ball after ball—
Wide of the mark or short are all;
But still the space is narrowing down:—
"We'll have him yet!" shouts Captain Town.

But now a scene surmised before;—
The stranger heaves his cargo o'er:
His iron hull is laden deep
With stores he finds he cannot keep.
Off float the boxes and the bales;
But even this expedient fails:

The lightened ship has much o'erthrown,
And still she cannot hold her own:
Straight onward, as though not to choose
To right or left an inch to lose,
While the sea after spuming churns,
A furlong more the cruiser earns.
The sailors cast their gloating eyes
Upon the drifting merchandise;
Then follow fagot, plank and bar,—
Tossed out the chaser's wheels to mar:
Meanwhile the breezes freshening come:
The hunted rogue has hope therefrom.

He scans his foe's light-drafted bulk,
And her extended breadth of hulk,
The broad wheel-houses, that retard
Advancing when headwinds are hard;
While his own ship, so sharp, he knows
Can readier pierce as gales oppose.
Adroitly acting on the thought,
His steamer to the wind is brought;
The foiled pursuer does the same;
But slowly loses on her game,
Which driving through in maddest force,
Successful strains his altered course:
In the gale's teeth his flight he shapes;
And with an oath the prize escapes!

A SEASIDE DREAM.

'Twas hours before the sundown boat
Would at that Tropic landing float;
And in a netted hammock flung,
I waited, sleeping as it swung;—
The vision to my memory clung.

In my bright villa on the peak,
　　A task is mine:
It is for thornless ease to seek,—
　　Lifelong recline.

My father drove laborious prow
　　Through China Sea;
With fortune came and made me vow
　　I'd idle be.

He placed me on this hazy cliff
    And decked my home;
Then stepped in his argosy's skiff,—
    Again to roam.

Away I marked him fleetly wear
    Towards far Mysore:
They told me soon a typhoon there
    A convoy tore;

Yet I 'gainst care and courier shut
    My heart and tower:
My father's dubious fate gave but
    A gloomy hour.

Eyes to my summer moon are raised
    Beyond the seas:
Gazing on her as I have gazed
    From grottoed ease.

We hear she has a God, and just;
    But cold and far:
They who have naught but Him to trust,
    Most wretched are.

The arm of flesh is warm and strong:
  What can be nigher?
It shall redress my every wrong,
  Win each desire.

With it my friend my heart's elate,
  Unvexed and free:
It shall console,—in every strait
  Deliver me.

The unconverted's eye they say
  Hard, glassy is:
Not so the Christian's; there's a ray
  Of grief in his.

Methinks I love him when he's bowed
  In chastenings low:
Though I am proud I hate the proud,
  I scorn their show:

And though they chant their rituals sweet,
  Commune and pray;
They shall be ashes 'neath his feet
  At Vengeance-Day.

I've walked to where immersed in sand
  On beaches far,

The bilging wrecks bird-haunted stand,
   With listed spar :

On them the water-shadows lone
   At noontide play ;
But men to sail and men to own,
   Are gone for aye.

What cares vain beauty that they lie
   On whimbreled shores ?
She flames in halls pretension high,
   While man adores :

And what to me their woe and loss ?—
   My purse is sure :
Their transient gains may flit across ;
   But mine endure.

While rifts of dust the splendor tame
   Of tapestry hem,
In high-lipped vase the nectars flame
   Like molten gem.

For as the years embrowned the frieze
   And dimmed the gold,
The lustre refuged here in these—
   My liquors old :

And so it is the happy sum
   Of all I do:
My joys no sooner fade than come
   In shape anew.

With filmy orb I lounge and note
   The wings of gulls;
The pennons which in distance float,
   And all that lulls.

O let the sweat of valleys grieve
   The man of toil;
My life shall flow as calm as eve,
   As perfumed oil;—

As free as the sun-glistening horse
   The pampas roves;
As smooth as crested chariots course
   Through palace groves.

One morning when I silent lay
   In oriel height;
Palled were the heavens in leaden grey,
   With base of light:

And there in sudden, bold define,
    What scene occurs—
A forest!—like the jagged line
    Of northern firs.

The horizon whereon it rose
    Is crowded black;
The mass approaches, larger grows,
    In forward track.

An aqueous murmur, gently loud,
    Its movements cause:
A dome is cloven in the cloud;
    The objects pause:

Then by that slanting glow I saw
    The vision plain:—
Ships of all time, from ocean's maw,
    Here sailed again!

Each class by many a plan and style
    And age, estranged;
Drawn up as though in curve and file,
    By admiral ranged.

There Cathay, Tyre and Denmark ply
    Their ancient oars:

And Britain's liners bristle high
  Their cannoned floors:

The galleon, trader, craft of steam,
  Malay malign;
And yachts of princes—all their gleam
  Consumed with brine.

By spell the rotten beams in place
  Are held as one;
As wires mount in study-case
  The skeleton.

Clusters on hull and tattered sail
  Convervoid green;
While down the masts of many trail
  Vines submarine.

The strengthening sun the heaven clears
  To wondrous day:
A sunlight lacking, it appears,
  A prismy ray.

Detached and vivid come o'erhead
  New Glooms opake;
Then in a voice remote and dread,
  The Wind-god spake:—

"Storms, show thy prey!"—each sep'rate
    Shade
Its own collects:
The phantom Tempests here parade
    Their phantom wrecks:

And while their clammy, briny smells
    About diffuse;
The host, melodious with its bells,
    The god reviews.

Grandly at unseen signal beck,
    Manœuvre all;
The thirsty birds a nimbus peck
    And showers fall:

Refreshed the ghostly messmen ope
    The wonted song,
The sailors' notes at chain and rope—
    Slow, wild and long.

They sing in turn; but when they meet
    In hap commune,
Combined their chorus shakes the fleet—
    A storm of tune.

Their flags the navies flaunt and dip,
   In passing speed :
I quickly see my father's ship,
   Her name I read.

The crew on reedy quarter keep
   A circling pace ;
While I with ten-fold vision peep
   In each man's face :

He is not there !—but that escape
   Can scarce console :
Death he has met in other shape
   Than blast or shoal.

Soon on my olden flowers and calm
   Dilates my eye ;
Upon my castled cliff I am,
   In oriel high ;

Above me bends his countenance
   With joyful tears :—
Unscathed it by shipwreck chance,
   But etched by years.

The sun upon the ocean quaffs
   His vesper wine ;

And, sure of future glory, laughs
   At his decline;

But rarer pageantry illumes
   Our garden cove;
In pomp centennial bursts and blooms
   The aloe grove.

Now, in our hour of strength and pride,
   We'll wisdom learn;
And land from off this dancing tide
   Before it turn:

We'll give our hearts and treasures up
   To Lord of all;
If need be share His earthly cup
   Of shame and gall.

We'll seek despairing ones to save,
   To help and soothe;
Make their crushed lives more sweetly brave,
   Their deathbeds smooth.

Long as our busy day protracts,
  His Word we'll spread :
He will accept our faithful acts,
  As He has said.

Here we've no song ; but hope for what
  Shall ne'er be dumb :
Here no continuing city—but
  Seek one to come.

My dream within a dream, is past :
The cutter waits for me at last ;
The straggling crew resume their ash ;
Impel with oft-recurring plash.
Poor children of the sea,—how due
What good I work commence with you !

THE ICEBERG.

There's in a region of my studied map,
    The Giant's home whom I from fancy draw:
His mother Greenland reared him in her lap—
    Patient 'mid polar night and cold and thaw:
    Rewarded when his wondrous strength she saw.

Aurora pleased him:—he revered her; and
    Absorbed the glory of her splendid eye:
She brushed his temples with her treacherous
        hand,
    Sent him adown the inviting ocean nigh—
    Like human Power to loom, dissolve and die.

Uncharted Teneriffe—stupendous isle
Unclaimed, ungarrisoned—a wandering Alp
Detached and venturous—an Iceberg lone
Drifts on the ocean! Heaped grotesque,

THE ICEBERG.

As by the fancy of a god at play, the crags
Teem with romance's emblems. Frost exhausts
His potent cunning; and the irised pomp,
Flamed in wild breadth upon the glassy steeps,
Is as though sunset gifted mantle here—
Nature heart-set to image out a King.

Frigates far beyond
The horizon below, the peak o'erlooks;
And, probing to unfathomed night, the draught
Explores the terrors of the nether waste,
Whose currents bear against the surface tides,
The bulk colossal that leagues coolness round.
While bubbly nebulæ interior halls
And cells, are charged with hyperborean air;
Where fairies or sprites embryo might dwell
In the eternal purity of cold:
So, held by flesh, the soul of heavenly breath
Awaits departure; as dissolving fast,
These wander up and on the sunshine burst,—
Fringing a rim of effervescent sea.

A bark becalmed is near. A hundred eyes
Are peering o'er the nettings; glancing up
The mighty altitude—from where upon the wave,
Swallowing its brine, the caverns monster-
    mouthed,

Fanged bright with icicles, yawn in mysteried
    depth—
To silvery ridges and the summit's crown
Of scintillating pinnacles that pierce
The sky with fragile fingers:—Sol o'er all
Flooding his glory. Everything is still
In the grand presence; vanity's suppressed
By grave emotion—wonder, awe and dread.

Water is gushing devious down the Berg,
As river down the cheek of distant mount.
A boulder vast and black is bedded near
The tranquil brim, and soon to fall therein—
Landmark and marvel to a future land;
But on a lower ledge a form of life!—
An Arctic bear stalks circumscribed and opes
Despairing roar.

The mass turns slow; and silently displays
A sight of horror—vestiges of some
Colliding ship impinged upon the ice:—
A torn-out stem with garniture of wreck;
Bowsprit and martingal, figurehead of gold,
Headrails and headstays, cutwater and bitts,
Breast-hooks and capstan brassed and anchor red;—
Conspicuous all. 'Twas some such tale as this:

THE ICEBERG.

The busy engines of a steamer kept
Through misty midnight a metallic hum.
The drowsy watch no peril dreamed; below
Lay the returning from the foreign tour.
Frothing in wake a mile of white abode
But the hid moon to sparkle. On the track before
Moves unperceived the Berg. In the hushed air
Are ghoulish whisperings, as though the deeps
Hist to each other—wistful for their prey.

As the war courser, roweled to the bone
On the repelling line of leveled steel,
Recoils upon his haunch with cloven throat,
Amid the shower of his own life-gore;—
So this arrested traverser is checked
By the ice-rock, 'mid the descent
Of splinters myriad; and quickly feels
The exultant ocean's inward-darted grasp
Cold in her vitals. Crowded sleepers roused,
In frantic panic seek unplanned escape;
Through cabin floor the pressing seas suffuse
The carpet cespitous; through portals surged,
They seize and buoy aloft the trinketry—
They drink the splendors of that long saloon—
They gnash against the ceiling. Then the plunge!
Above the bulwarks mount the boarding streams,

As wolves across a rent stockade—or as
The eager legions of besieging war,
Wheeled to the storming shock, tumultuous sweep
The escaladed rampart; and as o'er
The roaring rout, yet planted in its midst,
The doubtful standard holds precarious root—
So sways the royalmast to flaunt once more
Its pennant—ere above the diving truck,
And crushed or davit-foul or swamping boats,
The maelstrom spins, the thousand relics rise;
And struggling men in darkness clutch them round.

And morning came, as mornings often come
After our nights of woe—serene as e'er,
And innocently radiant—as unaware
Of what transpired meanwhile. The ortive sun
Inducts afresh the miracle of a day;
In confidence appears, in hope to touch
Anew his petted ship of yester-eve.
He sees her not; yet climbing, wider range
O'erlooks; and, more surprised, a wider still:
Then settling on the Berg he seems to say,
As the Almighty to the guilty Cain,
"Where is thy brother?" Now there came a
  cloud—
An interposing cloud athwart the disc;

THE ICEBERG.

And on the pile the shadow fell, while all about
Was luminous :—it was as though God frowned
On the Destroyer and abhorred its work ;
For as where'er a man may wander, sky
Keeps e'er above him ; even so 'tis vain,
In the sphered world's inclusion, to elude
Or move out from beneath His overwatching.

A child repines for its providing sire ;
A wife drops tears upon a miniature ;
A mother watches, with hand-shaded eyes,
Some one's return ; and all the little whirl—
The wonted whirl of hopes, alarms, despairs,
Transiently noises the overdue, the foundered, lost.
While the cold Iceberg
Stalks o'er the sea in silence : as the proud of earth—
The throned, the famous, and the beauteous too,
Course on impenetrably iced in self—
Thoughtless, regardless of the wrecks they cause.
But One said long ago, that like as wax
At fire wasteth, so let such as these,
Ungodly, perish by a present God ;
And thou O Berg ! when yonder sun
Exchanges temperate ray for torrid flame,

Then thou in lower latitude shalt melt!
Even now thy groan
Of verging dissolution rumbles forth—
As some sapped rib or glacial shield falls in;
And, like a battery's voice, shoots startling boom!

  The bark becalmed, from which the hundred
      eyes
Peered marveling up, now scents reviving breeze:
Her agitated jib distends, contracts,
Like a fawn's snuffing nostril. Seamen trim
To favorable angle every yard;
And watch each indication of the air.
Lo, what a crash of glittering ice behind!
Is the Berg toppling?—no: its crown is reft:—
The lofty diadem that frosting floods
Shot with prismatic beauty, and encast
On this their champion's brow, is shivered off—
Its gemmary debris hailstoning the deep;
And to a chaos of commingled dyes
Shatters the mirrored shimmering below.

  And softly as ourselves and past events
Recede each other from on Chronos' sea;—
Mark soon the level distance rolling out,
Like mazarine velvet from imperial loom,

THE ICEBERG.

Between the hieing ship and solemn Berg!
But mile to mile near doubled score extends,
Ere to the glass-trained eye the Ice-king all
Descends in ocean:—and above the tip
The skyline closes objectless and lone.

FINIS.

HYMN.

(From the Book of Common Prayer.)

Sovereign Ruler of the skies,
Ever gracious, ever wise;
All our times are in Thy hand:
All events at Thy command.

He that formed us in the womb,
He shall guide us to the tomb:
All our ways shall ever be
Ordered by His wise decree.

Times of sickness, times of health,
Blighting want and cheerful wealth;
All our pleasures, all our pains,
Come and end as God ordains.

May we always see Thy hand,
Still to Thee surrendered stand,
Know that Thou art God alone;
We and ours are all Thy own!

www.ingramcontent.com/pod-product-compliance
Lightning Source LLC
Chambersburg PA
CBHW032237080426
42735CB00008B/900